Aspirations
By
Annamarie Vickers-Skidmore

© 2014 Lulu Author. All rights reserved.
ISBN 978-1-291-82740-8

CHOOSE LIFE

FRIENDSHIP

What are friends?
People you can trust and you know they'll never let you down?
Or people that walk all over you and mess you around.

Who are friends?
School mates in the playground or people you know at home?
Or people that ignore you and leave you all alone.

Why are they friends?
Is it because you're generous and can take them picking on you?
Or is it because you're friendly and support them in everything they do.

So next time you think you've got a friend just stop and wonder why?
Your friendship makes you feel lost and you know you just can't cry.

Does your friend respect you for who you are?
Or do they only like you for what you can give.
Is your friendship really one-sided?
If they leave do you think you can live?

Well I'm telling you something right now, with all your strength you'll go on,
Leave your so-called friend that treats you like dirt, because your relationship's one big con.
You'll meet that special someone that treats you like a star,
Until you find that someone find out who you are.

Tonsillitis!

Tonsillitis, the horrible virus, whoever invented the word,
Whoever it was, is out of their mind and utterly absurd.
Tonsillitis, who needs the virus, not me for a start!
Your head is whirling, your throat is hurting and it feels like your being pulled apart.

Tonsillitis, I could strangle the person that ever invented that word,
You're stuck in bed and feel half dead and just can't get rid of Aunt Merd!
Tonsillitis, what a disgusting word, forever in bed with thoughts whirling through my head,
Oh please God please, I'm begging you, can't my sister have it instead.

Tonsillitis, don't say it again, I think I'm going insane,
Nobody wants to know me they think I'm a big pain,
Tonsillitis, oh when will it go, when will I see the world again,
Maybe tomorrow, maybe in a year!!
Will I ever be the same??

Tonsillitis, I've warned you once not to say it no more,
As far as I'm concerned you ghastly, nasty virus you can walk right out that door!!
Tonsillitis, I'm getting angry now, just go and leave me alone,
Just buzz off and away from here, hurt somebody else's jawbone.

Tonsillitis, I'm going to scream, how did I get in this mode,
My ears and eyes are hurting like mad, and I'm literally going to explode!!!
Tonsillitis, I'm feeling short sighted, oh why did I have to lie!
If I have to spend another day in this bed, I think I'm going to die!!!!

My Star

Silver is my cat and I love him very much,
He's just one big fluff ball and he's soft and silky to touch.

He really is a strange cat; he rolls around on the floor,
And when he wants to come in he decides to climb up the door.

He lies in front of the fire kicking his legs up in the air,
He shows absolutely everything, but he really doesn't care.

He's the laziest cat I have ever met and he doesn't like the cold,
He's sometimes disobedient but he has a heart of gold.

Sometimes I think he's mad because he pounces at things that aren't there,
He stalks along the ground, and growls just like a bear.

Sometimes he gets angry and lonely if we decide to go away,
But he's not always a charming cat if he decides to disobey.

In my eyes he is silver and shines just like a pearl,
But he's pitch black and we used to think he was a girl.

I adore him very much and when I hurt him I cry,
But I know one day I'll lose him and I'll have to say goodbye.

He'll join the stars in heaven all glittering in a line,
And I'll look up and see my Silver the brightest star to shine!

Hospital Nightmares

Stuck in a hospital,
With nothing to do,
I've not got a deadly disease,
And I don't think I've got the flu?

Sitting in a waiting room,
Is such a bore,
I'm here now with my brain in turmoil,
Wondering what's in store.

So I'm sitting here all alone,
Waiting for my call,
To see the lovely doctor,
And it's driving me up the wall.

What is she going to say?
Will she give me some pills!
Oh I'm dreading going into that room and all
the blooming hospital bills.

It's just like going to the dentist,
I'm going out of my mind,
I hate coming to the hospital,
It's always such a bind.

Well here comes the doctor,
She's calling my name,
I whisper my prayers under my breath,
I wish I never came.

HEAVEN SENT

A new life brought into the world,
A precious bundle to hold,
Somebody to care for and devote your love, to
keep your heart young when you grow old.

They depend on your life,
To nurture them into a sense of security,
To give them everything they'll ever need,
They'll always be your priority.

You're so proud of your bundle,
You want to show the babe off,
You live for the life of your child,
You panic when they cough.

You watch the bundle take its first step,
And laugh for the very first time,
The babe shares its simple first word and says
a new nursery rhyme.

You hope to be together forever,
To be there for every event,
To never miss a moment of their life,
You praise the gift you've been sent.

You want to wrap them in cotton wool,
To protect them from every distress,
But you know you can't hide them away from the world,
You offer your arms in caress.

When they get a job and their freedom,
And move into their own home,
Just think of your sweet little bundle,
And you'll never feel alone.

LIGHTS! CAMERA! ACTION!

The lights go down,
The show's about to start,
I bottle up the fears within with the constant beat of a racing heart.

There's so many strangers out there,
And they've come to see me,
I think I'm going to faint,
And I'm dieing for a wee!

I've rehearsed so many times,
Words are coming out of my ears,
What if I land on my bum?
I'll probably burst into tears.

What are those words?
"It'll be alright on the night",
Who are you trying to kid?
"Break a leg" Yeah right!

But I'm just being silly,
I will do this if it kills me,
I will prove to the world that I can!
Soon they will all see.

I'll go out there and reach for the stars,
Nothing can stop me now!
The audience will start to cheer,
As I start to take my bow.

They're clapping me and me alone,
And my heart begins to soar,
They're calling for an encore,
With my shoulders back and my head held high, I'll step through the stage door.

FOLLOWING MY DREAM

I didn't know whether to laugh,
I wasn't sure whether I'd cry,
But when they gave me that certificate,
I felt that I could fly.

My heart was beating madly,
I wondered if I'd shake,
I had to pinch myself hard to check that I was awake.

I didn't expect this,
I knew I wasn't a star,
But for the moment I could see my name in lights,
Above a Broadway show bar.

They said I was amazing,
That I sang really well,
I was so incredibly nervous,
That I couldn't even tell.

But what pleased me the most,
Is last night I won the fight,
I was no longer a nobody,
I was a person in my own right.

See I've never had much confidence,
A smile is easy to fake,
But when I stood on that theatre stage,
The world was mine to take.

SPARE A THOUGHT

People milling everywhere,
Going through life without a care.

They don't see the future,
Or what lies behind,
They'll wake up one morning,
Only to find:

They're all alone,
With no one to hold,
When the days are long,
And the nights are cold.

But we can change that,
At least we can try,
We need to kiss this lonely feeling goodbye.

So next time you see an old lady,
Remember to give her a smile,
Don't walk on by without saying a word,
Stop and talk awhile.

And when that old man,
Passes you by,
Give up some of your time to just say hi.

You're the generation,
On which the elderly can depend,
Whether you're young or old,
Everyone needs a friend.

MOVING ON

I'm moving on with my life,
I've decided to take the wheel,
I'm heading in a new direction,
What's happening seems unreal.

Becoming an adult is a scary thing,
I don't really know where to begin,
But I know I have to take the journey to
finding myself within.

I don't know what the future holds,
I'm scared of what lies ahead,
But with my friends and family around me,
I know there's nothing to dread.

Nothing in life comes easy,
I've learnt in my childhood years,
You have to strive for what you have,
And face up to your fears.

For all those tears I've cried,
For all those smiles I've shared,
I'm living my life just as I want,
With no expense spared.

I want to make something of myself,
I've gathered my survival kit,
Every happy moment and trial and tribulation,
Shows life is what you make it.

HOLDING ON

Back on my own,
Watching days go by,
Not knowing whether, to laugh or to cry.

We were so right,
Before we went so wrong,
Just wanting to know if I'll ever belong?

I thought you loved me,
Straight from the heart,
But in just one conversation,
You tore me apart.

You bruised my self esteem,
But I'm standing tall,
When you said goodbye,
I weathered the fall.

Now I'm back on my own,
And the sun will still shine,
And I'll find love again,
Further down the line.

Life will go on,
And the grass will continue to grow,
In time I'll forget that I loved you so.

LOVE LIFE

PIPKIN & I

Pipkin and I,
Went to sea,
It's quite a long journey,
But we'll be back by three.

Pipkin and I,
Went to the fair,
Pipkin challenged a grisly brown bear.

Pipkin and I,
Have lots of fun,
Underneath the blazing sun.

Pipkin and I,
Walk down the street,
Never knowing who we're likely to meet.

But Pipkin and I,
Have a thing that we share,
It's the love that we feel an emotion so rare.

Pipkin likes to travel,
But wherever he may go,
All I do is call his name,
And he'll come running back to me.

HOW CAN YOU TELL?

How can you tell if he loves you?
How do you know if he cares?
Is he all you dream off?
The answer to all your prayers?

How can you tell if he's thinking of you?
Are you the only thing on his mind?
Does he think you're a wimp and ugly?
Or does he think you're smart and kind.

How can you tell if there's another?
Someone else he adores?
Are you willing to be another notch on his bedpost?
Or do you want something more.

How can you tell if he respects you?
And likes you for what you are,
Are you stuck in a rut for the rest of your life?
Or will your relationship go far.

How can you tell if he needs you?
To be there for him all the time,
Will he take care of you and treat you like a lady?
By loving him are you committing a crime?

Hard to say goodbye

Why did you say goodbye?
Oh why did you go away?
There was so much left unsaid,
And so much I didn't say.

There's a dull ache here in my heart,
Where our friendship took hold and grew,
They'll never be another quite as kind-hearted
as you.

I know what it's like to feel lonely,
I know what it's like to feel blue,
I hope our friendship is strong enough to stop
this bond breaking in two.

It's really weird without you,
And all your teasing remarks,
But I promised I wouldn't cry,
On the day you said goodbye.

MOTHERLY LOVE

A mother is a rock,
You can lean upon,
When times are hard,
And nights are long.

A mother is the breath,
Of a silent breeze,
Her voice is the gentle sound of the falling leaves.

Her touch is the soft caress,
Of a butterfly,
She has the power to make you laugh,
And cry.

Your mother will always be your best friend,
An angel you know, you can always depend.

Her love knows no limits,
To her you're the Earth,
The one she has loved since the day of your birth.

So let all the world,
Unite and say,
We live for our Mum's,
On this happy day!

Love So Strong

We've been together for all these years,
Holding onto a love so strong.

We've had our ups and downs,
But love has seen us through,
I love the way you're mine,
I love every part of you.

We were once two people,
With a love so precious and new,
Now we are one body with a love so old and true.

You'll always be there for me,
In everything you do,
If we're ever apart,
Know I'll be thinking of you.

You're everything I'll ever need,
My world, my heart, my soul,
I'll always have you close to me when the nights are long and cold.

I will be yours forever,
Nothing could break this love,
This bond between us,
Was a gift sent from above.

THANK YOU

Thank you for being there,
When I needed you,
You held my hand through the old and the new.

You are my existence,
My guiding light,
You taught me the meaning,
Of what's wrong and what's right.

Thank you for loving me,
The way that you do,
You gave me all I needed,
You're my faith and my truth.

Thank you for the good times,
And the help through the bad,
Your shoulder to cry on whenever I am sad.

So I'm writing this poem.
To say thank you to you,
For the love that you gave and the things that you do.

I hope to be with you,
For many times to come,
So thank you for everything,
My darling mum!

PERFECT LOVE

You're my sunshine in the morning,
My starlight through the night,
You captured my heart without warning and
brightened up my life.

You're the reason I go on breathing,
When everything's falling apart,
But when you put your arm around me,
I feel your racing heart.

You say you'll never leave me,
That this time its forever,
That nothing could ever break us,
We were meant to be together.

You are my perfect love,
And right now you don't exist,
But someday you'll be real,
And I'll know what its like to be kissed.

A part of me wants to feel love,
Like I've never done before,
To sweep me of my feet,
And teach my heart to soar.

But really I just want a friend,
Who'll be there through the good and the bad,
To take my hand and guide me through the happy times and the sad.

Just somebody to listen,
When I have something to say,
Someone to come home to, to cuddle at the end of the day.

LOVE IS...

Love isn't always hearts and flowers,
It may not always be new,
But when I look into your eyes,
I can feel my love for you.

Being alone was never easy,
Sometimes life seemed hard,
But you came along and took my hand and
showed me the light from the dark.

I never knew I could feel this way,
I'm always asking why?
You came along and captured my heart,
When I thought love would pass me by.

You make me feel so special,
When you tell me that you care,
And when you're close beside me,
I love to know you're there.

I'm nothing that special,
I'm an ordinary girl,
But you showed me that you loved me when
you came into my world.

You make me feel safe,
In a world full of hate,
From the day that we met,
I knew it was fate.

Where life will take us,
I really don't know,
But we're in this together because my heart tells me so.

LOST

I feel like I'm in a maze,
And I don't know what to do,
Take this direction or the other I simply don't have a clue.

The pain I feel inside me threatens to take hold,
When I see her lying there she looks so frail and old.

I need her here beside me,
To hold my hand when I cry,
But she's slipping away from me when I'm not ready to say goodbye.

The feeling of being lost, I have nowhere to run,
I can't afford to breakdown, got to be strong for mum.

I just want her back where she belongs,
So we can nag each other and sing happy songs.

I'd give anything for extra time,
To tell her I love her so,
But big C has taken that away from me,
And I know she has to go.

I hope there's a place called heaven,
Where she can be happy and free,
And every now and again,
I hope she remembers me.

She'll always be in my heart through the good times and the bad,
She'll never leave my side when I'm happy or I'm sad.

When I look up to the sky,
And wonder what will be,
She'll be the brightest star watching over me.

ONE WISH

You are the air I breathe,
You're everything I need,
My head was telling me you're the one,
And my heart agreed.

Whenever you are near,
I always want to smile,
Whenever I feel down,
You hold me for a while.

When you hold my hand,
My heart takes wing,
I never knew what joy,
A simple touch could bring.

You pull me close,
With a tender kiss,
I never thought,
Life could be like this.

We have our ups and downs,
But all the time I know,
You're the reason for my existence,
And I could never let you go.

So I'm writing you this poem,
To say I love you so,
And even when we're apart,
My love for you will grow.

2 YEARS ON

Two years on,
And I know you're not here,
But I still feel you around me when I shed a tear.

I remember placing my hand in yours,
And the way we hugged so tight,
But then you were taken away from me,
And your heart gave up the fight.

In times of joy I can feel you there,
Your smile warm like the sun,
I hope that you are happy and proud,
Of the woman I've become.

In times of sadness,
I feel your tears soaking through my skin,
They echo in my heart,
And the storm starts to begin.

Everyone gets scared sometimes,
But then I feel you near,
The memory of your tender touch wipes away my fears.

And so the world kept turning,
And life went on to some degree,
New babies were born and people passed on,
But the world stood still for me.

I carry your memory in my heart,
Though it's not always clear to see,
In the air that I breathe and the ground beneath,
You'll always be a part of me.

LIVE LIFE

First Encounter

He stands there just watching me; I don't know what to say,
If I try to introduce myself he'll probably run away.

Everybody's scared of me and they're always really mean,
They think I'm white and mystical, so I really can't be seen.

I wish he would react,
But he just stands there and stares,
I try to smile and stand there with no uncertain cares.

He seems to have gone a deathly white; I hope he doesn't faint,
He keeps looking through me like I'm not here,
I'm going to make a complaint.

The boss never told me when I crossed over my life would be like this,
He could at least have made me an angel and given me a life of bliss.

Instead I'm stood here like a berk waiting for the moment to pass,
It's coming any minute the shatter of the glass.

I'm going to lose another friend,
Just because of how I look,
Here goes another one squealing like a duck.

I don't want to be a nothing; I just want to go home,
I'm fed up of being looked at,
I don't want to be alone.

What did I do to deserve this?
I sometimes skipped class,
I hate this screaming stuff,
I should have gone to mass.

BEYOND THE RAINBOW

Have you heard the tale?
Of the yellow, red and blue,
You may not believe me,
But the fairies say it's true.

Just walk through the archway,
And wonders you will see,
Of leprechauns a leaping,
One, two, three!

Just over the archway,
A little to the east,
There's said to be a pot of gold guarded by a beast.

In the far off meadows,
And on the banks of the stream,
If you look very carefully,
You'll see a distant gleam.

The fairies whisper through the night,
Of stories of the gold,
They say it holds secrets,
Never to be told.

The twinkling of the colours,
Shines down for all to see,
But the fantasies and magic,
Belong to only me.

CHANGING FACES

People stare as she walks down the street,
They giggle at her every stride,
They don't understand that they're breaking her heart,
She can run but she knows she can't hide.

The boys don't even look at her, nobody seems to care,
Other's smile sympathetically the smirks she just can't bare.

She lives in her world of fantasies,
Where she doesn't get called a freak,
She curls herself up in bed and cries herself to sleep.

Nobody knows her anymore,
They see what they want to see,
They don't see her dieing inside because of their cruelty.

People think she's abnormal,
They think she doesn't mind,
But she knows down deep in her heart,
They don't mean to be unkind.

She'll carry on with her life no matter what,
She won't deny that she's different,
She won't be something she's not.

If people only look further,
Deeper than her face,
They'll see a petrified child,
Not a living disgrace.

She waits for that person,
To take her into their home,
To show her the love she's never had,
The day she's no longer alone.

WHY?

Why did you leave me?
Why couldn't you stay?
My world fell apart as you were blown away.

You said you would love me forever and a day,
But you shattered my heart,
Now there's nothing to say.

I became just a shadow,
I didn't exist,
I never considered I'd be the bottom of the list.

You have your own life now,
That's what you said,
But why does that mean,
That our love is dead?

We were so close,
Right from the start,
Now were rocked to the core and miles apart.

You took the fuse,
And set it alight,
You left me in the dark whilst you're blinded by the light.

The explosion was violent,
The fallout immense,
The smoke isn't lifting,
And the fire's intense.

I feel like I've lost you,
Though you're easy to touch,
The bomb that hit us has taken too much.

___TOUCHED BY THE VOICE OF AN ANGEL___

There are lots of myths and stories,
That tell of the pale blue sky,
The holy place where God lives and all his
angels lie.

Nobody knows what angels are,
But I'll tell you my point of view,
They don't wear fluffy white gowns and halos,
They're just like me and you.

If you'd asked me a couple of days ago,
If I thought angels were true,
I would have told you plain and simple, that I
didn't have a clue.

But today something happened,
That made me change my mind,
I met someone in a café,
Who was sweet and charming and kind.

When he looked at me with his dazzling smile,
Straight away I knew,
I'd been touched by the voice of an angel,
Who disappeared into the blue.

LIVING A FANTASY

Your first love,
Your first kiss,
You never knew,
Love could be like this.

The way he smiles,
The way he speaks,
Makes your legs go wobbly and weak at the knees.

The everlasting beat of the heart,
Sends your stomach in a whirl and you swear you'll never part.

But the day will come,
When you go your separate ways,
And all you'll remember is those long, endless days.

The days he held you in his arms,
And never let you go,
What went wrong in that beautiful dream?
Your heart will never know.

FLYING HIGH

Life can be cruel sometimes,
When nothing seems to go right,
The journey doesn't come easy,
You have to strife to win the fight.

It's ok to feel scared and lonely,
Cos someone will always be around,
To take you in their arms whenever you feel down.

There will always be happy times and sad times too,
But you mustn't give up,
No matter what you do.

When people put you down,
The hardest thing is to walk on by,
Even though you're hurting inside they'll never see you cry.

You have to be true to yourself,
Discover your hopes and your dreams,
See the world through another's eyes,
Nothing is ever quite what it seems.

Whatever life brings to you, just take it in your stride,
You'll always be a stronger person after the long and bumpy ride.

People like to suggest the kind of person that I should be,
But as far as I'm concerned,
I'm happy just being me!

You can make a stand,
In any place near or far,
All you have to remember,
Is be true to who you are!

GUARDIAN ANGEL

Everyone is scared sometimes,
They try to face the world on their own,
But all you have to do is take my hand,
And you'll never be alone.

My heart is beating inside you,
My soul will always be yours,
When it feels like your dreams are ending,
I will help you open new doors.

You may not be able to see me,
But I will always be there,
My shoulders are your refuge,
On which your troubles you can bear.

My mission is to protect you,
From everything life can throw,
But be careful of the paths we take,
As we reap just what we sow.

My presence is always around you,
In everything you do,
Day or night I'm with you,
To make your dreams come true.

For I am your guardian angel,
And nothing's what you perceive,
I will always be watching over you,
No matter what you believe.

MEMORIES

Wish you were here for Christmas,
How can it be the same?
Tossing and turning all night, relentlessly
calling your name.

The snows beginning to fall,
I'm feeling cold inside,
Everyone tells me to move on,
God knows that I've tried.

I don't want to be without you,
The little things make me remember,
I can feel your hand in mine,
And hear the songs we sang together.

Your laughter echoes in the breeze,
Your image in the stars above,
You may no longer be at my side,
But I'll always feel your love.

Drifting Away

Sitting on a cloud,
Watching life pass through,
Remembering the days when it was just me and you.

The way we swore, we'd never leave,
Each other on our own,
I never thought that I would be so lost and so alone.

Oh why did you leave?
Do you even know?
The deepness of my soul and how I love you so.

You were the centre of my world,
You broke my heart into,
So I'm sitting on this lonely cloud watching time pass through.

ASPIRATIONS

I don't write fiction,
I go with the flow,
I use my ideas,
And write what I know.

I guess I don't know much,
As I'm only a teen,
But I've lived a few years,
And I know what I've seen.

Life isn't always perfect,
Sometimes it's terribly unfair,
But it all goes down on paper,
And my feelings are all laid bare.

It's easier to write the truth,
Than say the words out loud,
As people then don't judge you,
And you can face them strong and proud.

And as I become older,
My ideas will expand,
I will face life's hurdles,
And begin to understand.

And when I'm old and grey,
I can relive my feelings again,
And know the memories stored in my heart,
were written first by my pen.